PRACTICAL COACHING SERIES

THE ART AND SCIENCE OF EFFECTIVE COMMUNICATION

How to Listen with Empathy, Talk with Confidence, and Become a Charismatic Person

By Daniel Hudson

Additionally, the information in the following pages is intended only for informational purposes and should thus be thought of as universal. As befitting its nature, it is presented without assurance regarding its prolonged validity or interim quality. Trademarks that are mentioned are done without written consent and can in no way be considered an endorsement from the trademark holder.

TABLE OF CONTENTS

INTRODUCTION

Congratulations on downloading *The Art and Science of Effective Communication: How to Listen with Empathy, Talk with Confidence and Become a Charismatic Person*, and thank you for doing so.

Often, when we speak to others, we end up feeling exhausted and misunderstood. It is almost guaranteed that the people we are talking to feel the same. One of the most common complaints in communication is feeling misunderstood. This is because we generally do not pay full attention to one another. The highest form of communication is listening, and the highest level of listening is understanding.

The following chapters will focus on the differences between speaking and hearing, and true communication. The first chapters will discuss how to develop listening skills that aid in understanding, as well as how to express yourself openly. Once we have discussed the basics of effective communication, you will learn how to handle some communication challenges, and how to project a charming presence. Finally, you will discover the secrets in establishing and maintaining effective communication in specific situations. Each chapter also includes practical exercises to help you in developing your skills and mastering effective communication.

There are plenty of books on this subject on the market, thanks again for choosing this one. Every effort was made to ensure it is full of useful information. Please enjoy!

Chapter 1: Developing Empathic Listening Habits

After spending an entire day in conversation with various people, we can feel stressed, exhausted, and more importantly, misunderstood. When considering that many, if not most, people feel similar, it is easy to see how arguments over insignificant issues can commonly occur. With the use of effective empathic listening, we can help alleviate some of this discord. We can ensure that others feel understood, and become more effective listeners as well.

First, let's take a look at the reasons why communication may break down or may not be effective in the first place. *Stephen R. Covey*, an American educator, developed a listening continuum that identifies **five levels of listening**. The continuum is the basis of our discussion for the remainder of this chapter.

Most often, we use one of the first four levels of listening. These first four levels are not effective.

The first level is *ignoring*. Ignoring occurs when the speaker is speaking, but the listener is not listening. This can be due to the listener not focusing on the speaker whether deliberate or not. With this level of listening, communication does not move forward because the issue has not been heard. Results of this communication breakdown are often arguments based on the speaker's feelings of not being heard or understood.

Level two on the continuum is *pretending*. Pretending most often occurs when the listener multitasks or finds something more important than what the speaker is saying. Pretend listeners make generalized comments or sympathetic sounds to make it look like they are paying attention. Pretend listening can also be deemed patronizing as it allows the speakers to believe that they have been heard. As far as understanding or problem-solving goes, pretending does not allow communication to progress, because again, the message has not been heard. A breakdown of communication occurs here as well. The results often include issues in future conversations that may have centered on the topic discussed while pretending to listen.

At times, when listening to a speaker, we hear parts of the whole. This is due to *selective listening*, the third level on the continuum. Sometimes, we only hear part of the message that piqued our interest. Selective listening can also happen when the listener interrupts the speaker or tries to complete thoughts for the speaker. This is the first level where communication is occurring but is problematic because listeners process things through their own experiences. The listeners only hear what sounds important to them, or may even think that they understand because of prior experiences. As long as we hold on to our own thoughts and experiences, or even try to insert them into what the speaker is saying, we will not be able to understand. Again, at this level, understanding has not been achieved and it is not possible for a resolution to be reached.

Attentive listening is the final lower form of listening. Attentive listeners often believe they are truly listening. While that may be true, they still have not reached the level of understanding.

With *attentive listening*, listeners are still filtering everything through their own experiences. They may mean well in saying that they understand how the speaker feels or that they too have gone through something similar. But the main issue here is that no one can really know how another person feels. We know how we felt or reacted in a similar experience, but it could never be the exact same way for another.

The last and biggest step we need to do to overcome this and break through to the highest level of listening is to stop sympathizing with a speaker. This can be very confusing and may seem counterintuitive, but until listeners can overcome their own feelings and biases, they cannot truly understand.

What is Empathic listening?

Empathic listening is best described as the most effective way of listening to improve understanding and to increase the level of trust in a relationship. Mediators are some of the best empathic listeners. They often have the best results in alleviating misunderstanding or miscommunication. Empathic listening creates an environment where the speaker truly feels heard and understood. Empathic listening uses not only the brain but also the heart. Listeners must use their hearts to really understand what they are being told. One of the biggest payoffs of empathic listening is seeing people drop their armors and defenses. Being a recipient of empathic listening also causes the speaker to be a prepared listener.

A major positive outcome of empathic listening is that speakers may be able to solve things on their own. Often, a speaker may just need to be in the presence of an empathic listener to independently come to his or her own satisfying conclusion.

As an empathic listener, you have the ability to empower the speaker just by listening and understanding. Listening empathically is not easy. It may also not feel natural in the beginning, but it can be practiced. The more you practice listening with empathy, the easier and more natural it will become. Empathic listening can be used in every conversation, in any relationship, every single day. Utilizing the highest form of listening will make your relationships and eventually, your life, better.

When listening empathically, it is important to remember that you are listening with an intention to understand what is being told. You do not need to agree or relate to it, but rather, you just want to understand what you are hearing. Once you understand, you may need to continue listening until the speaker feels understood. This is a very important point.

The key to empathic listening is making the speaker feel understood. Sometimes they may need to continue speaking to feel that way. Make sure you are being empathic, and not just sympathetic. When you sympathize with someone, there is a level of judgment involved as you are comparing your experiences to that of the speaker's. You are unconsciously deciding on the degree of sympathy to offer. To be empathic, you must emotionally understand another person's point of view. Listen to understand the meaning and the feelings behind the words. Remember to watch out for nonverbal cues like behavior. These can often clue you in on the underlying emotions if you have difficulty understanding from the words alone.

Empathy in a listener can be felt by a speaker. The conveyance of empathy may mean any tension will gradually lighten. The environment may feel more secure.

When listening empathically, a response is not always needed. But if you do respond, it is important to remember that there is a difference between acknowledging what was said and how it was felt. You do not have to agree with what was said. By acknowledging, you are in no way giving approval or agreement. Rather, you are simply acknowledging the feeling behind the words spoken. Withholding judgment is the main component of empathic listening. Acknowledging words and feelings is empowering to both the speaker and the listener. Both parties also avoid leaving the conversation with negative feelings.

Open-ended questions also serve well in helping the listener to understand, and the speaker to feel understood. Asking open-ended questions lets the listener receive more information to better grasp emotions conveyed. Another proactive way to respond is to ask for clarification. It acts as a checkpoint and an assurance to the speaker that the listener hears and does understand. On the listener's part, it ensures that they also understand and are on the right listening track. Finally, it allows the speaker to feel that they are understood, or it provides them the option to explain further.

Practical Exercises to Develop Empathic Listening

Let's try some exercises to develop your empathic listening skills. The next time you are in a conversation, think through this checklist. You may even choose to have a practice conversation with a close friend or someone you are quite comfortable with.

Practice will only help you become a better listener, and to use empathic listening more automatically.

- *Be completely focused on the speaker. Do not try to think of a response.*
- *Remove all personal thoughts, including similar experiences, on the matter. Refrain from telling the speaker you know how they feel.*
- *Withhold any disagreement from what you hear. Focus on understanding the words and feelings.*
- *Resist the urge to mimic or parrot what has been said to you.*
- *Let go of any attempts to control the conversation.*
- *Listen to the words. Listen to the feelings behind the words. Listen to any hidden need behind the words.*
- *Deal only with the speaker's reality.*
- *If needed, ask for clarification. You may also wish to ask an open-ended question.*

- *Listen until the person has finished speaking and has felt heard and understood.*
- *Consider carefully any response if needed. If a response is appropriate, remember to acknowledge what was said.*

Once you have completed your first conversation using empathic listening, take a moment to reflect on the experience. Ask yourself the following questions.

- *How did this conversation vary from those you typically have? How did it compare? What was the atmosphere like?*
- *How did you feel like the listener? Assess your mood and feelings. How did the speaker react to the way you listened? Did this vary from prior experiences with this same person?*
- *What were the results? On what note did the conversation end? Did the speaker feel as though you understood what they were saying? Do you feel that you understood the speaker?*

CHAPTER 2: THE ABILITY TO EXPRESS YOURSELF FREELY

Having developed the skill of empathic listening, the next step is learning how to express yourself freely, openly, and with confidence. There are many reasons why people have difficulty expressing themselves freely. They may feel too reserved. They may think that their thoughts are not important. They may even simply want to avoid any confrontation. You can overcome these with a few skills and a bit of practice. You will need to draw on and extend some skills you learned in chapter one.

As you have learned, acknowledging a feeling or a thought does not automatically grant approval or agreement. This is true for your own thoughts and feelings as well. This chapter will help you learn to acknowledge, label, and express your own thoughts and feelings, without analyzing or rationalizing them too deeply. You will learn how to be confident in any conversation, allowing you to make more connections. You might just find yourself enjoying conversation more.

Listen to yourself

You are now taking on the role of a speaker, but not entirely shedding the role of a *listener*. This is because you must still be able to listen to yourself internally. The key component to expressing yourself freely is to be able to listen and understand <u>yourself</u>.

It is healthy to be able to put your feelings into words, and yet, this is a very difficult task for many to do. It is necessary to understand your own thoughts and feelings to ensure that you will be understood by others. Recognizing and labeling emotions are an imperative part of learning to express yourself openly at will.

Feeling safe and free to express yourself will rid the atmosphere of negativity. Speaking about your thoughts and feelings will allow you to view them in a more positive light, especially if they used to make you feel worried or fearful. It takes courage to speak out and state your opinions and feelings to others. But saying things out loud will be more fulfilling than keeping them bottled. You may find that you have a great solution to a problem. You may inspire others to speak freely. You will see your feelings, worries, and fears as more authentic, and yet, bear less weight internally. This leaves you feeling freer, light, and most importantly, understood.

To express yourself freely to others, you must first be able to internally recognize your thoughts and feelings. It may be helpful to meditate or sit quietly on your own. Clear your mind of any prior assumptions or thoughts of how you should feel. Listen to your internal thoughts. Focus on how you feel, and take note of your reactions to these feelings. Pay attention to how your body feels and the behaviors you might display. Keeping tabs on all these feelings and reactions will help you as you begin speaking freely to others.

Identification

The next step is to acknowledge and *label* your feelings. Just as with empathic listening, you must free your mind from judgment. Recognize that you do not have to explore why you have that feeling or even make excuses for it.

It's important to understand how you feel <u>without</u> questioning or rationalizing your feelings. Anything you feel is valid. Try not to overthink things. Just take note of the feelings, acknowledge them, and give them a label. It is imperative to understand that emotions are natural and they do not make you weaker. You can take control of your feelings and emotions by giving them a label. After that, you will be more confident in expressing yourself to others.

When acknowledging your thoughts, it can be beneficial to think in terms of "*I.*" An example would be telling yourself "*I feel this way*," and to then give a name to that feeling. There is no need to rationalize your feelings. You have a right to your thoughts, feelings, and emotions.

Sometimes it may take time to understand your own internalizations. When speaking in response to another person, an immediate reply is not always necessary. In fact, it may even be beneficial to take time to listen to your inner dialogue. If you find it difficult to take note of how you feel and think, it may be helpful to keep a journal.

In this journal, you can record your thoughts and feelings about any situation. Using "*I statements*" will be most beneficial here, because the journal will serve as a bridge between acknowledging and labeling your thoughts and feelings to yourself. Eventually, you will have the ability to speak more openly and freely to others.

Just as with empathic listening, speaking freely can be achieved with practice. With repetition, it will become more natural and automatic. When you have developed the skill of speaking openly and with confidence, your daily life will improve, lowering feelings of stress and anxiety. You will also have the added benefit of knowing that you made yourself understood in every situation you are.

Express yourself

You are now ready to express yourself outwardly. When speaking freely with others, it is important to remain calm and be respectful to yourself and your listener. This will make you feel less anxious, and be more positive and satisfied with the conversation. You will also be able to avoid arguments and be confident that you were able to express yourself concisely.

Use the first person to tell how you feel. For example, "*I feel this way when this happens.*" Using "*I statements*" helps avoid placing blame. It does not put any pressure on the listener to argue back. This is a healthy way to put your feelings and thoughts into words. It pushes you to be more clear and concise in your speech.

It is also important to take into consideration the aspect of *respect* when you are speaking. You do not want to belittle yourself or your feelings in any way, but you also want to make sure your listener feels respected as well. This means you treat yourself and your listener with <u>equal respect</u>.

Simply state your thoughts, including feelings or emotions that you have internally acknowledged and labeled, on a given matter. It is important not to feel defensive at any feedback you may receive. A key in learning to speak freely is to take any response as constructive criticism. It is okay to tell the listener that you need to give more information to be understood. If you state your opinion and still do not feel understood, it is acceptable to clarify your position. This requires just a simple restatement or extension of your thoughts. When holding conversations, it is healthy to keep in mind that what you think, feel, and say is valid and deserving of respect and understanding.

Practical Exercise to Develop Speaking Skills

This exercise will help you develop skills in speaking freely. It is an exercise that will aid you in identifying and maintaining mutual respect within a group while speaking with confidence.

It is essential that this exercise is done with a small group of three to four people, including yourself. Individual exercise is not going to be truly effective. Choose close friends or people you have trusting relationships for this practice session. Decide on a topic for discussion. It may be helpful to prepare a few index cards with potential topics ahead of time. Reflect on the following checklist and then state your opinion, thoughts, or feelings on the topic.

- *Identify and acknowledge your feelings. Give them a label.*

- *Drop any defenses you may feel on the topic.*
- *Remember that what you have to say is important and worthy of being heard.*
- *Reflect on the fact that your feelings deserve validity, understanding, and respect.*
- *Use "I statements" like, "I think" or "I feel."*
- *Speak calmly, and with respect for your opinion and for your listeners.*

After you have spoken freely, ask other participants to reflect on the levels of respect they felt.

- *Did the listeners feel respected as you spoke?*
- *Did the listeners feel you gave respect to yourself when you spoke?*
- *Did the listeners feel that the levels of respect were equal or unbalanced in any way?*

Contemplate the following questions about your experience.

- *How clearly was I understood?*
- *Was I respected when I spoke?*
- *Was I respectful to the others involved?*
- *Are there any changes I could make for improvement the next time I speak freely?*

At this point, you may wish to switch perspectives. Someone else in the group can take a turn as the speaker while you rate the attempt at speaking freely. Rating others will help you easily identify levels of respect when in a conversation. You may rotate roles as many times as needed until everyone feels that they had enough practice.

Chapter 3: Handling Various Communication Challenges

In the previous chapters, you have learned how to develop your skills in effective communication. You had the chance to practice listening empathically and speaking freely. There are several common hindrances to effective communication that you may encounter. In this chapter, some of these hurdles will be presented, along with ways to overcome them.

The first obstacle to effective communication is **distractions**. This can be the result of listeners not paying attention, a lack of interest on the topic at hand, and other types of disruptive interference. Let's focus first on what the speaker can do to help overcome these distractions.

The speaker can reduce irrelevant information if he detects a lack of interest in the audience. In doing so, the speaker can be more concise. Inattention means the focus is diverted to somewhere else. The speaker can attempt to identify the distraction, such as noises or interruptions, and try to eliminate it. As for the listeners, some simple planning can help against any distraction. A listener should make the conscious decision to focus on the speaker and the speech. Avoid interrupting the speaker. Questions should be asked at the appropriate time. If easily distracted, take precautions such as sitting away from doors or windows, silencing or turning off cell phones, or jotting down a few notes while listening to aid in their focus on the speaker.

The next type of challenges is **differences in viewpoints**. These differences include culture, gender, social status, and age, which may prompt contention within a conversation.

Insensitivity may arise in these types of situations. The lack of a common background may create contrasting points of view. For both the speaker and the listener, it is crucial that they educate themselves on potential differences. For example, what is considered polite may vary between countries and cultures.

Simply being aware of these differences may avoid derailments to communication. Both the speaker and listener should remind themselves to be calm and emphatic. They should use "I statements" to mitigate any issue. A reset of communication may be needed in some cases. A short break may be taken before regrouping. Something as simple and quick as a set of calming breathing techniques may be enough to alleviate any tension. Although many people share similar experiences, their interpretation may differ from one other. Consider the idea that people will have different experiences on the location of the items in the same room as them. Everyone could be in the same room at the same time, but their experiences would vary solely on the location of their seat, and the vantage point offered to them. Because of this, it is imperative for the speaker to start from a point relevant to the listener, so communication can flourish and have a common point of understanding. The speaker can also try to create a connection based on the listener's schema, or prior knowledge of the topic. This may provide the needed point to create a common understanding. In turn, the listener can make connections between what they already know and any new information they are getting. The listener must let go of all assumptions and prior experiences to meet the speaker at a point where effective communication may take place.

Some communication difficulties can be eliminated before they even become an issue. For example, a person may be planning to speak in front of a group. In this group, an individual speaks a different language or has a hearing disability. A simple solution is to provide a translator who can aid in understanding. Conversely, a speaker with speech difficulty can provide a translator to the group. In some cases, the use of visual communication can be also very effective in aiding in understanding. For example, using photos in an informal conversation among friends, or a PowerPoint presentation for a speech to a large company. As a speaker, it is important to always use correct grammar to be understood effectively.

Another difficulty that can be prevented is **nervousness about freely sharing thoughts in front of others**. This can be resolved by internally checking, acknowledging and labeling your feelings, as well as practicing how a conversation or speech may go. A little bit of planning can go a long way in preventing possible speech difficulties.

Another challenge in effective communication falls under **misunderstandings and miscommunications**. The best way to avoid miscommunication is for both the speaker and the listener to be focused on speaking freely and listening empathically. A speaker should be clear in communicating thoughts, ideas, feelings, expectations, emotions, and opinions. The speaker should discuss any expectations to bring everyone on the same page. As previously mentioned, equal respect for yourself and for your listeners is necessary. If there is a miscommunication issue, everyone involved should quickly try to discover the problem and get back on track as soon as possible.

Miscommunication can potentially unravel all efforts to keep an effective conversation flowing. As such, both the speaker and the listener should do a little internal listening. If you have a concern, state the issue concisely, while projecting respect for yourself and others. If a misunderstanding arises, the speaker should try restating thoughts in a different manner. It is also better to immediately get the conversation back on track. This would likely save time and avoid unneeded stress for everyone involved.

The last hurdle is **mutual respect** for both the speaker and the listener. This refers back to chapter two about balancing the respect between a speaker and a listener.

The speaker needs to be clear about the objective. Be sensitive and understanding to the needs of the listener, while still maintaining respect for one's self. Refrain from using professional jargon. Instead, use layman's terms so everyone has an equal level of understanding. If there are concernings on the lack of feedback, the speaker should feel free to ask for it. This can be an opportunity for the speaker to ask a listener to restate what they heard and determine if the point got across. This also can allow the speaker to evaluate the effectiveness of his speech and determine if further clarification is needed.

Summing It All Up

Some final key components to remember are as follows:

- *Think before speaking. Avoid interrupting. Pause before reacting. Determine if a response is needed and helpful in the current situation. If the answer is no, use self-control to let the speaker move on.*

- *As a speaker, be brief and clear. Be aware of nonverbal cues that the audience may display. These cues may include facial expressions, shuffling, or fidgeting. By taking note of these, you can have a clue on whether they understand or not, and can adjust appropriately.*

- *In the cases of both the speaker and the listener, remember to be professional, kind, polite, and courteous at all times. Kindness and respect will go a long way in creating an environment that is conducive to effective communication.*

Practical Exercise to Overcome Communication Challenges

The following exercise can be helpful in any communication issue. Reflect on the benefits of writing feelings in a journal with the use of *"I statements."* We will expound those benefits here.

Any time a difficulty arises, jot down some quick notes in your journal. You may choose to complete the exercise at the time of the issue or at your leisure. The most important aspect of this activity is honesty to one's self. Remember that it is natural to experience emotions whether positive, negative or a mixture of both. If you are unsure that you can be calm in a given situation, it is a good idea to brainstorm in your journal. An immediate response is often not required, and you can take the time to develop an appropriate answer, as opposed to derailing effective communication at that moment.

- *State in writing what the issue is. Determine where the breakdown in communication occurred.*

- *Label your feelings and list them in your journal. You can also use this section to reflect on the equality of respect. Do you feel that both speaker and listener had equal levels of respect? Does this impact communication positively or negatively? Could this be improved in any way?*

- *Brainstorm appropriate and helpful ways to resolve the issue at hand. These will be helpful in the current situation, as guide you for future conversations as you hone your skills to become a master of communication.*

- *Try writing various ways that you might state this resolution in a conversation or a meeting.*
- *If this is an ongoing conversation, choose one of the resolutions, and present it by speaking freely.*
- *If the conversation has ended, use this list of brainstormed ideas as a reminder of appropriate ways that you may respond in the future for an overall improvement in communication.*

Chapter 4: Improving Your Charismatic Qualities

Charismatic people have the innate ability to magnetically draw others. They project an *aura* that others find pleasing to be around. While some people naturally have charisma, it can also be learned and practiced. Now that you are developing your effective communication skills, it will be even easier to improve your natural charismatic qualities.

This chapter will break down the characteristics that tend to draw people in. It also includes a practical exercise to improve your own qualities, making communication easier and more effective by simply changing the way you are perceived by others.

The most important aspect of being a charismatic person is being ***a confident communicator regardless of the setting***. Having excellent interpersonal communication skills will allow you to be confident in yourself and make others feel at ease. As mentioned in the previous chapters, an effective listener practices empathy. In speaking freely, it is important to remain assertive, positive, and optimistic, without showing signs of arrogance. Always show your most authentic and positive side. Do your best to also bring out the most positive aspects of your listeners. This will allow the other person to leave the conversation with a positive experience, and positive feeling toward you.

To project charisma, pay attention to the following points:

- *Draw interest by speaking freely and with confidence.*

- *Be knowledgeable about a broad range of topics, and maintain an equality of interest.*

- *Be understanding what others are also saying. Be sure not to pass judgment, and do not worry about thinking of a response as they speak.*

- *Show others that you have interest by asking questions of an open-ended nature. Inquiring about the feelings and opinions of others will let them feel that you are interested. Be considerate and treat others well.*

- *Remember details about the people you meet, particularly their names. Allowing positive experiences with you goes a long way.*

- *Communicate your own thoughts and feelings clearly. Be assertive in your speech while maintaining an honest and humble persona. Remember to acknowledge and label any emotions that you are feeling during a conversation.*

- *To take this one step further, acknowledge and label the feelings of others to cultivate a true level of understanding.*

Another key component in improving your charismatic qualities is **body language**. This encompasses the way you hold yourself, your gestures, your facial expressions, and how you make eye contact. To exude charisma, it is important to maintain a body language that is relaxed, open, and inviting. You want to give off an *inclusive aura*. Develop the use of open body language. Maintain a good posture. Stand straight and tall to project confidence. Refrain from crossing your arms, standing in a hunched manner, or fidgeting, as these are nonverbal cues that you are not inviting communication.

Open body language includes a relaxed stance with arms at ease, and a calm, positive facial expression. Practice being approachable, starting at smile at others when greeting or bidding farewell. When you are speaking or listening to a person, maintain eye contact, smile when appropriate, and show them that they have your full attention at all times. Listen deeply for understanding. Do not be afraid to be passionate, enthusiastic, confident, and optimistic when you choose to speak. This will help you earn the respect and trust of others.

A charismatic person can **pay attention** and **act on social cues**. Observe those you converse with, and notice the nuances. Take note of their facial expressions and their body language. These clues will assist you in understanding the feelings behind the words that you are hearing. Subtly imitating the body language of your conversation partner can assist in developing trust. This can be done by mirroring certain gesture they may make, or by responding with similar facial expressions. Always do your best to treat others fairly. Keep in mind that fair is not always interchangeable with equal. Some people may require more time for you to listen, while others may need more encouragement to feel confident in their abilities to contribute to the conversation.

Speak at a **_relaxed, open_**, and **_friendly pace that maintains interest_**. Remember to always maintain respect your own thoughts and your listeners' as well. Prepare a mental list of potential conversation starters. It will help if you keep up with current events. It is also useful to be knowledgeable about their interests and willingness to discuss these.

A few examples of good conversation starters are classic literature, community service, or an interest in a certain type of music. Try your best to be warm and considerate to everyone you interact with. Genuine compliments are always appreciated. You can focus on what the speaker is passionate about and letting them know that you can tell they really care. Always take a brief moment to think before speaking. Do not be afraid to ask for clarifications, if needed. Do not give in to the urge to say something just to fill the silence. It is perfectly acceptable for a brief lull in the conversation. Take a moment to allow your conversation partner to finish speaking, then, absorb what was said and formulate your reply. Run your response through your mind before speaking. Take each chance to respond as an opportunity to show the other person your authentic self. Remember that you have control over the way you want to be perceived.

Practical Tips to Boost Confidence

People with charisma exude confidence. To put your best self forward, there are a few things you can do to prepare.

- *Being well-rested and eating healthily is the foundation of your self-confidence.*
- *It is important to dress well and comfortably for the occasion.*
  - *You can give a quick boost to your confidence by wearing your favorite clothing or styling yourself in a way that makes you feel good*
  - *Feeling good will allow you to act in a more positive manner. It lets you be more open and makes others feel more at ease around you.*
- *In order to support any conversation, it is important to be generally well-read and knowledgeable about a multitude of topics. However there's also an easy way to be ready for small talk - staying up to date on news and current events.*
- *Do not rely on alcohol or caffeine for charisma. Instead, draw on the qualities that you already possess to strengthen your charismatic development.*

Keep in mind that it is not necessary to be a naturally outgoing person to exude charisma. If you are more reserved, focus on giving your complete attention and listening empathically. Remember, that your personal flavor of charisma may lie in your ability to *make someone feel understood* or in your *capacity to observe social cues*. It is not necessary to flaunt any specific qualities. The true key to exuding charisma is making others feel positive about themselves. This is best done by being an interested and attentive listener. Remember to balance this display of interest by being able to confidently speak freely yourself. You will be well on your way to developing your charisma.

Practical Exercise to Develop Charisma

What follows below is a two-part exercise to aid you in developing your charismatic qualities. By practicing, you will be able to show your best qualities with ease and develop your own brand of charisma.

- *Start by listing the positive traits that you already possess in the same journal you have been using for these exercises so far. These are the traits that you will show to exude the most positive and authentic version of yourself to others.*

- *While standing in front of a mirror or sitting in front of a video camera, practice speaking about any topic of your choice. Pay specific attention to maintaining eye contact with yourself and to the posture that you are presenting. Take note of any body language or gestures that you use often. Keep in mind that you are only looking at physical cues for charisma. You may wish to record these observations in your journal. You can make a note of the things that you have done well, that portrayed you as a charismatic person, and that you may wish to incorporate into your persona. Also, reflect on things that you may wish to improve upon in the future or that may require more practice for you to feel comfortable. You can repeat this exercise as many times as you would like.*

- *With the use of a video camera or a voice recorder, practice speaking about one of your interests or a current event. Remember to pause in order to assess, acknowledge, and label any feelings you might have on the topic. Speak freely while confidently expressing yourself and your viewpoint. Then, listen back to the recording. Focus only on how you sound. Take notes on the sound of your voice. Pay attention to the following:*
    - *Is the speed of your speech easy to follow?*
    - *How does the sound of your voice make you feel?*
    - *Does the cadence allow for interest while still being open and friendly? Do you sound confident and self-assured?*
    - *What do you like about how your voice sounds? Are there any changes or improvements you would like to make in order to project more charisma through the sound of your voice?*

- *Repeat this practice as often as needed.*

Once you feel that you have had enough practice, take these positive traits you have discovered, and begin displaying them at the forefront during social interactions. In your journal, reflect on conversations you have participated in. Determine any improvements that you have made and make note of any changes that you wish to make in the way. Continue to practice and improve effective communication and charisma with this exercise as well as those from the previous chapters. With practice and determination, you **will** become a master of effective communication.

CHAPTER 5: EFFECTIVE COMMUNICATION WITHIN SPECIFIC RELATIONSHIPS

In the previous chapters, you have learned how to develop your skills to become an effective communicator. The final part of becoming truly effective in all aspects of communication is to make use of your skills within specific relationship scenarios. In this chapter, we will delve into three common areas where we want to develop relationships based on effective communication.

Working Relationships

Good communication within the workplace fosters a better working environment that is more conducive to employee productivity. With effective communication guidelines in place, employees will understand expectations. There will be ongoing discussions of strategies and resolutions. This creates a more goal-oriented team that will be more productive. Better communication in the workplace also means better relationships among employees. A more satisfying work experience can also drive productivity and increase the employee retention rate.

The majority of misunderstandings or miscommunications in the workplace stem from a lack of effective communication. The use of *empathic listening* and *assertive speaking* in the workplace can nearly eliminate these misunderstandings, and also provides a framework for conflict resolution. Empathic listening can make a real difference in every workplace from meeting rooms to factory floors to classrooms. Its consistent use among employees, managers, and clients will decrease the potential for misunderstandings and create an overall better working experience for all involved.

Practical Exercise to Improve Communication in Working Relationships

A good training tool for effective communication in the workplace is the **empathy circle**. An empathy circle gives employees the chance to practice empathic listening and (with time) make it more organic for the workplace culture. The following is a description of how an empathy circle works.

- *Empathy circles work best with a group of four participants. When working with a larger company, the group can be broken down into smaller clusters for this exercise to take place.*

- *Within each small group, each member is assigned a role. The first member will be the speaker, the next member will be the active listener, and the remaining members will be silent listeners.*

- *It is best to have a topic ready to assign to the groups. You may also wish to assign a side for each group member to take on the assigned topic.*

- *The person who is assigned the role of speaker begins to talk about the topic to the active listener. The speaker and active listener should maintain eye contact throughout this part of the exercise. The active listener listens until the speaker feels fully understood. The active listener should not interrupt or pass judgment, but may ask for clarification if needed or try to make a restatement to the speaker to ensure understanding. The silent listeners only listen at this point and observe the interactions between the speaker and the listener.*

- *At the time that the speaker feels completely understood, it is time to switch roles. The active listener becomes the new speaker. A new topic may be assigned at this time. The former speaker now becomes a silent listener and one of the silent listeners takes on the role of active listener.*

- *This exercise continues until each person has had a chance to play each role. In closing out this exercise, there should be time allotted for employees to give thoughts and make observations about how this type of effective communication will work better for the company.*

Personal Relationships

Effective communication within our personal relationships allows us to have a deeper understanding of one another and to spend less time in arguments or debates. We are able to experience a bond based entirely on trust and understanding. The ability to have strong and effective communication with those we love the most leads to a higher overall satisfaction with the relationship.

Key components of effective communication within a personal relationship are *the ability to state needs and desires*. And the ability to *listen for understanding* even if you do not agree with each other. The addition of these two traits will lengthen any personal relationship.

Practical Tips for Effective Communication in Personal Relationships

- *When speaking with a partner, be sure that both parties have their full attention on the conversation. Create a specific time for discussions. There should be no cell phones or television for distractions.*
- *Body language is especially important for communication in personal relationships:*
  - *Partners should maintain eye contact for a good portion of any discussion.*
  - *It is beneficial for both partners to try to maintain relaxed and neutral facial expressions throughout the conversation.*

- - *It is especially important that neither person appears threatening or feels threatened by the body language of the other.*
- *Personal relationships are a great place for the use of "I statements" in effective communication. You may wish to refer back to chapter two for a refresher on "I statements." It is helpful for each person in the relationship to use language that does not place blame.*
- *There should be no interruptions as each person gets to speak until they feel understood. The listener needs to remember to listen to the words and the feelings behind them. As each person takes a turn as the listener, they should acknowledge the feelings and understand the perspective of their partner.*
- *Open-ended questions are a great way to keep discussions going.*

Ultimately, each person is responsible for their thoughts and behavior in the relationship and in every aspect of communication. The partners have to work together, and sometimes compromise to determine what is best for the relationship.

Practical Exercise to Improve Communication in Personal Relationships

Relationships take work. The following exercise can be used in a relationship where communication has not been effective or has deteriorated over time. This exercise can be used in any relationship involving two people. While it may seem strange and unnatural in the beginning, this exercise will ensure that the partners build good foundational skills to overcome basic communication barriers.

In this exercise, each person has a chance to tell about their day.

- *Start small. Set a timer for five minutes.*

- *The first person has this time to speak freely. The second person takes this time to be an active listener. The listener should not interrupt, should not pass judgment, and should not be thinking of a reply. The listener should be fully engaged in hearing the words and understanding the feelings and perspective behind what is being spoken to them.*

- *It is now the time for the partners to switch roles. The listener is now the speaker, and the speaker becomes the active listener. Reset the timer for another five minutes.*

- *The second person now has this time to speak freely. The first person uses this time to be the active listener. The same rules apply here as in the first round.*

- *This exercise can be used as often as needed, even on a daily basis. You may wish to work on adding time as needed, or even eliminate the timer eventually, and just focus on sharing with one another.*

Family Relationships

The last type of relationship we will discuss is the one between *parents and children*. Effective communication with children can make everyday life infinitely easier. It is also crucial in the development of children. Children imitate what they see. Our job in modeling effective communication will have a great impact on how children communicate with their parents, as well as others, in the present and in the future.

The first and the most critical step in developing effective communication with your children is to **always be available**. If your child is speaking to you, try to stop at what you are doing, listen to them, acknowledge their feelings, and understand their point of view.

Encourage your child to communicate with you. Even when they are still babies, speak to them often. It does not matter if you are just narrating what you are doing. This sets a precedence of communication. Be interested in what your child has to tell you. When they are young, they share with you what is important in their lives. Take the opportunity to set up a *foundation of trust*. This will pay off as they develop into teenagers and adults.

Practical Tips for Effective Communication with Children

- *Just as with adults, you have pay close attention to your child's body language. This can tell you more than on what they want to say.*
- *Always make sure that your child has finished speaking before responding.*
- *If they have questions, answer honestly. If you do not know the answer, say so and find the answer together. Show how to speak with assurance and respect.*
- *Label feelings for your children if they are having difficulty in doing so. Help your child discuss emotions, instead of them lashing it out. Be prepared to respond empathically to a range of emotions.*
- *Avoid placing blame or becoming angry when communicating with your children:*
  - *Work on solving problems together. This does not only help resolve the current issue but lays the groundwork for peaceful resolutions in the future, when older children and teenagers may hold a different viewpoint or opinion.*

- *You should both be able to state your opinions and respect one another. Effective communication is the key to a healthy relationship between parents and children.*

Practical Exercise to Improve Communication with Children

For this final exercise, we will focus on building effective communication and healthy relationships with children. While it may seem very basic, the meaning of this exercise is really profound. The goal is to allow each person in the family to understand that what they think and feel is <u>valid</u>. This is the foundation of your family's successful communication.

This exercise can be used on a daily basis. A perfect time to implement this practice would be during dinner time.

- *Bring a small timer with you to the dinner table.*

- *Each person in the family gets a set amount of time, perhaps three minutes, to speak about anything they want.*

- *The first person has the set amount of time to freely speak. Everyone else at the table takes on the role of an active listener. Once the timer goes off, this is the time that others can ask questions. You may wish to put a time limit on the questions as well, perhaps one to two minutes, before moving on and allowing the next person their chance to speak.*

- *Each person at the table gets a turn to be the speaker. You may cycle through the members of the family as many times as you wish until everyone has had a chance to speak.*

CONCLUSION

Thank you for making it through to the end of ***The Art and Science of Effective Communication: How to Listen with Empathy, Talk with Confidence, and Become a Charismatic Person***. Let's hope it was informative and able to provide you with all the tools you need to achieve your goals.

Remember, reaching the end of the book means you now have all the basic knowledge to be a master communicator. Be sure that you are mindful of your role in all aspects of communication.

The next step is to start practicing and implementing the skills you have developed in your daily life! Effective communication is always a work in progress. Therefore, my final words of advice for you:

- *Refresh and strengthen your expertise by revisiting the exercises included in this book as often as needed.*
- *Keep track of your improvements, strengths, and weaknesses in your journal.*
- *Enjoy the knowledge and understanding you gain from truly listening to others in your life.*
- *Remember that anything you think or feel is valid, and you have the right to express this.*

- *Get out in the world and show everyone your authentic self in the most positive way you would like to be perceived.*
- *You have charisma, don't be afraid to use it!*

Developing your best communication skills will help you excel in all areas of relationships you'll experience in life. And I wish you all the best in each of these areas!

Finally, if you found this book useful in any way, a review on Amazon is always appreciated!

www.ingramcontent.com/pod-product-compliance
Lightning Source LLC
Chambersburg PA
CBHW051129250726
48655CB00007B/2960